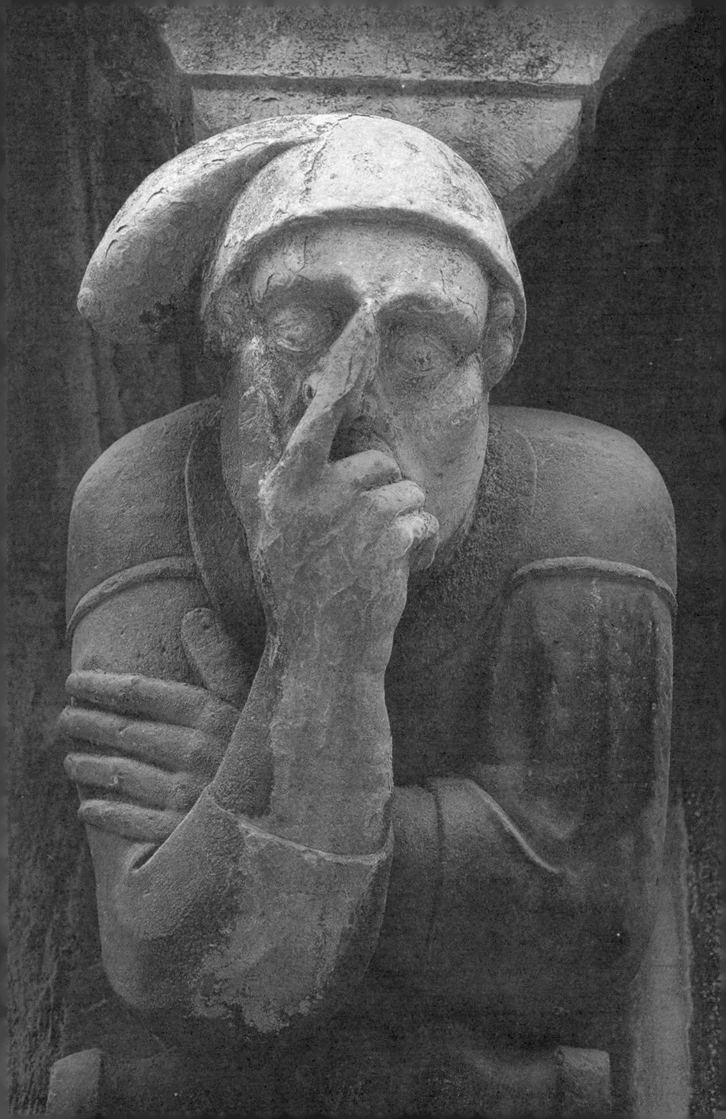

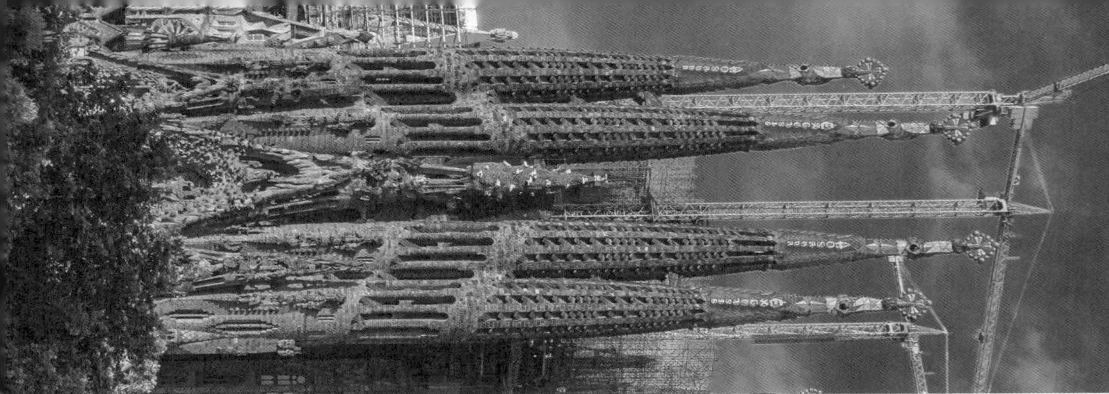

© Triangle Postals SL
Sant Lluís, Menorca
Tel. +34 971 150 451
triangle@triangle.cat
www.triangle.cat

© Text: Albert Carreras and Pilar Pifarré
© Photography: Pere Vivas
© Cover illustration: David Martínez
Publishing direction: Ricard Pla
Graphic design: Joan Colomer
Layout: Vador Minobis
Translation: Mark Waudby
Printed by: Gráficas San Sadurní 5-2018
Printed in Barcelona
DL: Me-351-2018
ISBN: 978-84-8478-808-9

Albert Carreras and Pilar Pifarré
have written:

Catalonia explained to visitors

A small land that is a blend of scenery, peoples, cultures, arts and identities. And ready to make lasting friendships and show people its wonders.

Little
Red
Books
Triangle Books

Introduction

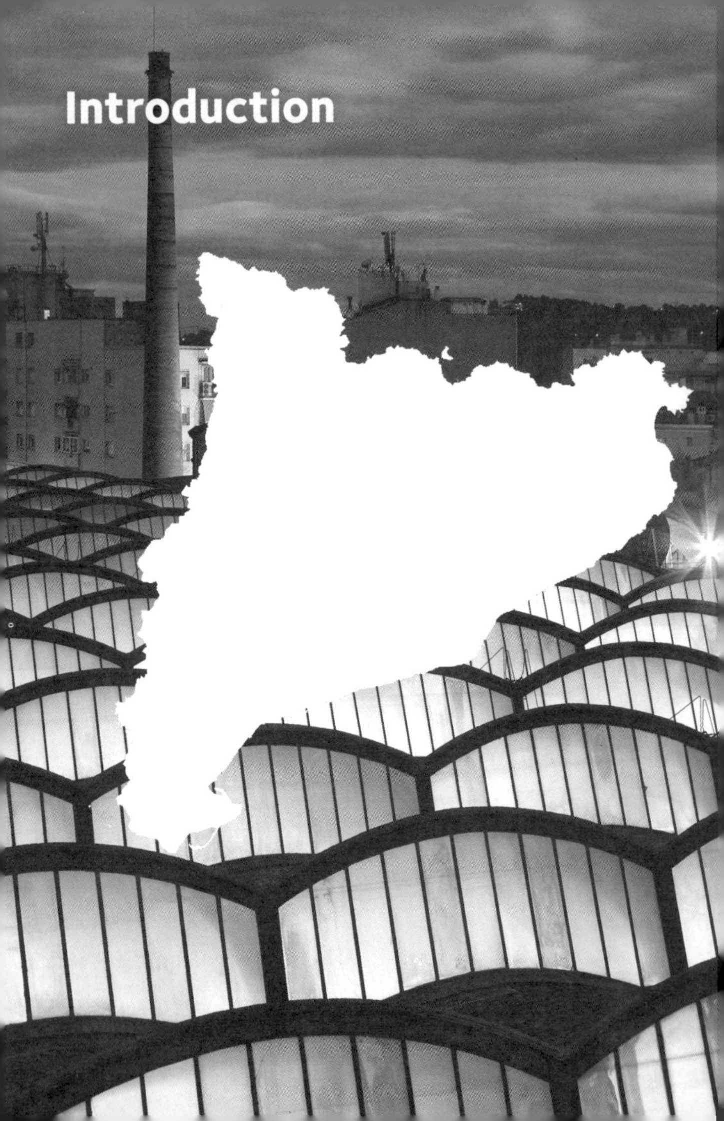

Catalonia is a triangle

with two sides that are similar in size — in the north, the Pyrenees and the border with France, and in the west, the boundary with Aragon and the Valencian Region — and a long hypotenuse, in the east, facing the Mediterranean. In the centre of the hypotenuse lies Barcelona, the capital of Catalonia.

Visitors to Catalonia used to be mainly attracted to the long hypotenuse of the coast, and still flock there in their millions today. Since the 1992 Olympic Games, increasing numbers have come to Barcelona. There is also a growing interest in the whole area inside the triangle. The entire region, with its 7.5 million inhabitants, welcomes more than 18,000,000 visitors a year.

Catalonia is an intensely political region. For many Catalans it is a nation without a state. For many Spaniards it is an autonomous region, like the others in Spain, but where the people are always grumbling. Catalonia has its own language — Catalan — and seeks to make its presence felt throughout the world with its own distinctive identity.

Barcelona has always been one of the cities in Catalonia that people knew about, but it was the Olympic Games that really put it into the spotlight. Barcelona's football team, FC Barcelona, or Barça, is world famous and the main football club in the Catalan capital. For many, it is the best team in the world. However, Catalonia remained a relatively unknown quantity, except to those tourists keen to explore the region they were visiting. Catalonia really put itself on the map with the demonstration held on 11th September 2012, when millions of people called for Catalan independence, and those held in subsequent years. Since then, journalists from media outlets around the world have reported from the city. The consultation process and subsequent referendum about Catalan independence, both of them banned by the Spanish government, and the declaration of independence and the republic by the Catalan Parliament, have put Catalonia firmly on the world map. Now Catalonia is known as a region with its own identity.

What is Catalonia like?

If we stick to the figures and remain objective — which we're not going to do here — we would say that Catalonia covers an area of 32,137 km^2, with a population of 7.5 million inhabitants and a

GDP of more than 210,000 million euros. It is an autonomous community within the Kingdom of Spain, with Barcelona as its capital. In terms of surface area, Catalonia is very similar to Belgium (30,528 km^2). Its population is similar to Hong Kong's, and somewhere between that of Switzerland, Quebec and Bulgaria. Its GDP is the same as Scotland's, and higher than it is in Greece, Portugal, Ireland, Chile and Finland. Catalonia is a Spanish autonomous community but almost half its inhabitants want to be independent. Barcelona isn't an issue: it belongs to everyone.

Geographically, Catalonia is a region in south-west Europe, in the north-east of the Iberian Peninsula, on the Mediterranean coast. It has a mild climate, which attracts holidaymakers in their droves throughout the year, and is a draw for highly qualified professionals from around the world who settle here permanently. It is also a welcoming place that has provided a home for generations of migrants who have come here in search of work and a better future over the last century.

Catalonia is European. Very European. Its history is quintessentially European. It has all the ingredients of many other European countries. The first human settlements can be traced back thousands of years. Its early-Neolithic settlers were the first in a series of peoples, such as the Iberians, with their own identity. The region was colonised by the Phoenicians, the Greeks and, more successfully and more permanently, the Romans. It was the Romans who shaped the region, and its peoples. Theirs is an enduring footprint. The balance of Roman Catalonia was upset by invasions from the north, which are referred to as "barbarian" (in line with the Romans' view of events), but were actually spearheaded by the same peoples who moved across Europe between the 3rd and 7th centuries of the Christian era. The region converted to Christianity at the same time as the entire Roman Empire. In the 8th century, the southern peoples — the Arabs — occupied most of the Catalan territory, with the exception of the valleys of the Pyrenees. The region played an active role in Charlemagne's empire at the end of the 8th century giving rise to the dynasties of the counts who governed what came to be known as Catalonia. The Christians had occupied the land under Arab rule by the middle of the 12th century. During the medieval era, Catalonia established its own political system, the County of Barcelona, which had its own parliament, or Corts, and became a model of medieval government. It became part of a wider kingdom — the Crown of Aragon — and developed extensive trade links throughout the Mediterranean, leaving its imprint on all the great islands in the western Mediterranean (except Corsica), Naples, and, to a lesser extent, Greece and Turkey. Like the rest of Europe, it also suffered the Black Death and the resulting decline in population. In the 15th century, Catalonia was involved in a number of civil wars which brought an end to the feudal exploitation of the peasant classes. Having become a region with a peasant class that was almost free, it was heavily resettled by the French (or Occitanians, to be more precise) in the 16th and 17th centuries. From 1640 to 1714, it made several attempts to become independent from the crown that also ruled Castile. Catalonia was defeated in 1714, and left without its own institutions. It went on to focus on work and business and prospered in the 18th century. Like the rest of Spain, it was occupied by Napoleon and became a province in the Napoleonic Empire between 1812 and 1814. In the middle of the 19th century, it witnessed three civil wars between the liberals (who were in favour of the parliamentary monarchy) and the Carlists (who supported the absolute monarchy of Carlos V) in the midst of a vibrant industrial revolution, the most southern one in Europe. In the 20th century, Catalonia didn't take part in the great European wars. After a long and painful civil war, it was plunged into a dictatorship that originated in the European fascist movements that had grown up between the wars. For decades it was sidelined from European history and events, but, when the dictatorship ended, its desire to become part of the new political Europe, constituted as the European Economic Community, met with a broad consensus.

Catalonia is European and Mediterranean. It is one of the most dynamic places in southern Europe and on the Mediterranean coast. It has cultural, political and economic ambitions. It has the ability to host world-class events, like the 1992 Olympic Games, and develop ambitious community projects, including new political structures (the Mancomunitat, or Commonwealth, of the four provincial councils of Catalonia, between 1914 and 1923; the Republican government of Catalonia, the Generalitat, a region with its own autonomy statute, between 1931 and 1939; the autonomous government reinstated in 1977; and, latterly, a potential republic in its own right).

Catalonia is an industrious, thrifty region. Its hard-working character has yielded a well-established labour base. Its early industrialisation, the most widespread and advanced in southern Europe and across the Mediterranean, has made it a revolutionary, left-wing region with a strong trade union movement, which readily takes to the streets to demonstrate, and chases utopias. It attracted revolutionaries from around the world during the Spanish Civil War (1936-1939), but it had already interested utopian socialists, anarchists, social democrats and communists of all kinds from the 1830s to the 1930s. It provided a refuge for exiles and was a magnet for spies during the Great War. It has again attracted radicals from all over the world, at a time when globalisation is being challenged, and shown tolerance and open mindedness to dissidents of all political colours and countries. The Catalans own awareness that they are dissidents with regards to the rest of Spain, has paved the way for this ideological and social openness. Catalonia is a place that shows solidarity and, over the past 30 years, has adopted the most children and given birth to the least.

Its hard-working character has yielded a hard-working bourgeoisie. Like the rest of northern Europe, Catalonia's bourgeoisie drew on the Calvinist ethos of hard work and thrift. Calvinism never took root in Catalonia in the strict sense of the word, but the fact that the region didn't have its own state, and was too far away to receive any favours from central government, meant that the paths to personal progress were restricted to hard work, private professional and business concerns, and to saving, a great deal of saving. This hard-working bourgeoisie was embodied by the hundreds and hundreds of families who, in one way or another, spearheaded the industrial revolution in Catalonia. Manufacturers, many manufacturers, all with their own factories.

Barcelona's new district, the Eixample, which provided a showcase for the region's home-grown art nouveau, *modernisme*, was the result of this new social structure. Every manufacturer wanted their own handsome building in the Eixample that would show off their prosperity, but which they could also use as collateral when times were hard and also as an investment opportunity. This district is an architectural treasure trove that still amazes cultured visitors from around the world. Although many people have tried, driven by a desire to make easy money through speculation, they haven't been able to destroy this vast heritage, which bears witness to the brilliance and scope of the industrial revolution in Catalonia. Following the city's successful bid to host the 1992 Olympics, Barcelona City Council launched an initiative to clean up the façades of its buildings. An architectural heritage of great aesthetic beauty began to emerge from beneath the layer of soot clinging to the walls of the houses. Most of these art nouveau, or *modernista*, buildings are found in Barcelona, but there are also many examples around Catalonia. They echo a cultural and artistic pride that is inextricably linked to the cultural renaissance, the *Renaixença*, that defined the Catalan national consciousness.

Catalonia's readiness to absorb new influences and ideas has made it a hotbed of creativity. Catalonia excels in many areas where there is no language barrier, including gastronomy, medicine, sport, painting, music, sculpture and the arts in general.

It is proud of its own language, which hasn't been absorbed by the official language, Spanish. As a dynamic society, with its own bourgeoisie and middle classes, Catalan has been a sign of distinction and a means of social advancement. This, together with a strong inner unity, has allowed it to survive the worst times of persecution and contempt. It remains to be seen if Catalan can hold its own against the soft power of the English language…

There are many Catalonias

We talk about Catalonia as if it were a monolithic entity. Nothing could be further from the truth. There are many Catalonias but they all have something in common: for instance, the football team, Barça. A good place to start classifying these different Catalonias is to distinguish between urban and rural Catalonia. Rural Catalonia is embodied by vast natural landscapes, particularly the mountains of the Pyrenees, the massifs in the foothills of the Pyrenees and the mountain ranges cutting through the centre of the region. There are also miles and miles of woodland, sweeping views, and counties of breathtaking beauty, such as the Vall d'Aran, Cerdanya, Berguedà, Ripollès and Garrotxa, as well as the Solsonès and the Terres de Lleida, and the mountains of the Terres de l'Ebre. Rural Catalonia is extremely wary of urban Catalonia, which "destroys" everything when it moves in from Barcelona and its metropolitan area.

Rural Catalonia is the cornerstone of the basic structures of the Catalan economy and families. Its centrepiece is the farmhouse, or *masia*, the home and workplace of farming families. The more successful and better off they are, the bigger and more beautiful their houses. These families are the descendants of the end of feudalism in Catalonia at the end of the 15th century, and the Catalan inheritance law which prioritises the heir. In years gone by, the eldest son would inherit the family estate and had to compensate his brothers and sisters. Farming dynasties have been able to preserve, generation after generation, their houses which formed the core of their estates. Now that agriculture and livestock farming are in decline, many of these *masias* have been converted into restaurants or hotels, opening them up to visitors. The *masia* is the symbol of this world. You can find them everywhere, in prime locations, built of solid stone and blending perfectly into the landscape. An outstanding work of art reflects the transition from the traditional to the modern while bearing witness to the way of life that bound the *masias* together: Joan Miró's painting, *The Farm* (1921-22). This is the greatest tribute by the urban world to the rural world. Curiously enough, the image is reproduced in reverse in another of the founding works of modern painting: Picasso's cubist *The Factory at Horta d'Ebre* (1909). It shows a factory with a chimney (which didn't really exist because the building was in fact a mill), symbolising the prestige of modernity of the age, in the middle of a lush Mediterranean landscape.

Coastal and inland Catalonia. The coast stands for innovation. The inland areas stand for tradition. The coast is open to foreign visitors and contact with the outside world, while the inland areas remain relatively unexplored and are more popular with Catalans. This contrast has always been reflected in the clash between liberals and Carlists. The mass influx of tourists who are only interested in the coast has stirred up old conflicts and long-standing resentments.

Traditional and creative Catalonia. Like many other places, there are parts of Catalonia where tradition means everything, and young people socialise by engaging in time-honoured rituals, games and festivities. Catalan has a rich folklore which has been revived and promoted following the reinstatement of democracy and devolved government. The *sardana*, the national dance of

Catalonia, probably originated in Ancient Greece and remains an affirmation of Catalan identity solidly rooted in tradition. It involves men and women, dancing in a circle holding hands, keeping time with their feet.

Castells, are human towers that can reach up to ten tiers and have been documented since the 18th century in the Penedès. Their displays are accompanied by specially composed music and have become a tradition that brings together young and old alike, while attracting new members of the community who love taking part in this fun and inclusive activity. Human towers have been awarded Intangible Heritage status by UNESCO.

Traditional festivals have gained in popularity. From the Patum in Berga to Carnival in Sitges and Vilanova, or bull running in the Terres l'Ebre, together with a whole host of festivals featuring parades of giants, pipers, drummers, and even people firing blunderbusses, as well as other activities that reflect Catalonia's popular culture. Many young Catalans socialise through these deeply rooted traditions and they are great fun for kids too. However, some young people choose to take part in creative activities of a different kind.

Catalonia has a plethora of musicians, artists, actors, directors, filmmakers, circus artists, and now digital creators, who view the new traditionalism from a critical distance (but, once again, the football team, Barça, binds them together). The cult of creativity has spread with great success to the field of gastronomy, which has been a successful way of shifting from tradition to creativity. The leadership of Ferran Adrià, who created a huge, and generous, school at El Bulli, has made a real difference and forged a style that the new culinary leaders have reproduced and multiplied with great success. There are now many restaurants that can surprise, captivate and satisfy their diners. Leading chefs have met with widespread acclaim from the public, in some cases worldwide, as is the case with Ferran Adrià and the Roca brothers. They attract talent from around the world as places to hone their skills at the cutting edge of the profession. They have revolutionised each and every one of the meals that can be served at the table, from tapas to desserts. Catalan patisserie, which was always of a high standard, is now brimming with irresistible ideas that are hard to compare with their equivalents around the world.

A Catalonia that is made up of so many Catalonias, always offers an attractive side to its visitors. Catalonia brings a lot of variety and little uniformity: this is the geographical bedrock of Catalan individualism. It can even be felt in the climate: every corner of Catalonia has a different climate.

All these factors make it the ideal place to enjoy many different experiences in a physically small space — 32,000 km². There's no time to get bored. No experience can be repeated often enough or exists on such a large scale that it becomes overwhelming. Catalonia is a land of variety. This means it can't be reduced to a single landscape or city, to a single landmark or a single experience. In order to understand it, you have to explore its sheer variety, which is its distinguishing feature.

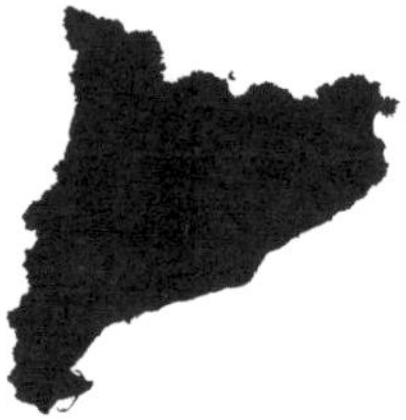

The Catalan triangle

The triangle we mentioned at the beginning provides us with the first physical and visual confirmation of Catalonia's variety. The following pages will follow the sides and interior of the triangle in search of the things that will help us discover the polyhedric, polymorphic, polysemic and eternally captivating essence of Catalonia. We'll begin with the long hypotenuse, the Catalonia with its beaches, which has attracted tourists for many years. Next we'll focus on the north-eastern tip of Catalonia, the area stretching from Girona to Cadaqués. From this tip of the Catalan triangle, we'll follow one of its sides — the Pyrenees — and continue, through Andorra, to the other angle where you'll find the Vall d'Aran and Vall de Boí, nestling in the heart of the Pyrenean mountain range. Afterwards, we'll head down the other side of the triangle, to the Mediterranean, where the mouth of the river Ebro flows out into its wide delta. Once we have explored the outer limits of the triangle, we'll take in a bird's-eye view of the most important inland areas. Next, we'll return to the coastal hypotenuse, paying particular attention to the towns and cities, and end at the city at the centre of the hypotenuse: Barcelona.

A land of beaches

When Europeans started going to the beach at the end of the 19th century, well-heeled Catalans — the region's bourgeoisie — began buying summer holiday homes in the villages on the coast. Barcelonians could go to Sitges, Masnou, Premià or Vilassar, which were all well served by trains. As time went by, people started to discover better beaches, but their inaccessibility prevented

Catalan summer holidaymakers from inland areas going there and spoiling them. S'Agaró, in the heart of the Costa Brava, was developed as a seaside resort in the 1920s and 30s and became the finest example of high-end, beach tourism.

The tourists, who began arriving in Catalonia after Europe had recovered from the Second World War, were certainly attracted by its beaches. The most highly prized were the coves along the Costa Brava, followed by the beaches in the Maresme, Castelldefels and Sitges. As tourist numbers increased, all the beaches along the Catalan coast began to fill up. The most accessible ones were the first, including those in the Maresme and on the Costa Daurada, followed by less accessible ones. The Costa Brava was completely overrun with a few exceptions.

Catalan beaches are of the highest quality, with clean, temperate waters, and sands that are comfortable underfoot and open to everyone. This is almost unique in Europe. For instance, not all the beaches in Italy allow public access.

While foreign tourists have made Catalan beaches world famous, the locals have been avid beachgoers too. During the transition from the dictatorship to democracy, the new democratic town councils on the coast invested a great deal of money in cleaning up the beaches, providing services (showers, toilets, waste collection, restaurants, bars and car parks) and stabilising the erosion of the shore, which had been easily washed away by autumn and winter storms. The beaches are currently one of the main focuses of community and political life and every town does its utmost to receive the best quality ratings. Media transparency has made the towns extremely competitive. In those areas where the coast was occupied by factories, such as Barcelona and its surrounding area, the beaches reclaimed for the community have offered affordable luxury with a broad appeal that has formed the basis of the local community's satisfaction with their amenities and local government representatives. When Barcelona opened up its coastline it was a great success for the people spearheading the transformation. This is what mayor Pasqual Maragall achieved through the city's Olympic bid. The same phenomenon has occurred in neighbouring towns like Badalona, which has gone from having no beach at all to having one of the largest beaches in Catalonia.

The traditional beaches, like the ones on the Costa Daurada, the Maresme, and the Costa Brava, remain just as beautiful but they are now facing strong competition. The overall result is a continuing improvement that needs to satisfy the demands of increasingly choosy visitors and locals. For instance, seafront promenades have been built everywhere, running alongside the beaches and providing pleasant places to stroll. They have met with immediate success. The seafronts in the coastal towns have become their great urban parks.

In recent years, the available beaches have filled up making it necessary to create new ones, particularly in Barcelona. These are the most successful, due to their central location and ease of access. Be that as it may, you can still find unspoilt beaches in the Ebro Delta. In fact, there used to be no beaches on the delta. However, due to a series of circumstances that we will look at later, it now has some 40 kilometres of top-quality sands. On the southernmost tip of Catalonia, there is a great reserve of long sandy beaches of the kind that have attracted visitors to Catalonia for almost a century.

Put in a nutshell, to a large extent, the current prosperity of Catalonia is due to its beaches which, all along the hypotenuse of the Catalan triangle, attract countless visitors every year, starting with locals, followed by city dwellers (from Barcelona, Madrid and Zaragoza), Catalans from the inland areas and, lastly, visitors from abroad, starting with the French, followed by the British, Germans, Italians and Dutch. In fact, increasing numbers of visitors come from further afield. It is important to remember that the local residents are the main users of the beaches. During the summer, the shopkeepers on the Costa Brava can only dream of closing their shops at lunchtime to go to the beach. The beach isn't only considered an economic way of life, but a general way of life too. The people who live there truly love it. They are well aware of this gift from nature.

On the northernmost tip, the Costa Brava offers the most beautiful coves. These smaller beaches, enclosed by cliffs and woodland, offer spectacular scenery and a variety of forms. From Blanes to Portbou you can enjoy countless coves and sweeping beaches (such as Pals or the Gulf of Roses). Most of them are linked by the coastal paths once used by guards and smugglers and connect many of the coastal villages. The best way to discover the spectacular natural scenery of the Costa Brava is to walk along its coastal paths. Although some of the beaches are crowded, such as Lloret de Mar and Platja d'Aro, you're more likely to come across peaceful coves and a few secluded ones off the beaten track. The Costa Brava continues to offer some of the finest coastal landscapes in the Mediterranean.

Between Girona and Cadaqués

On the north-eastern tip of Catalonia we find the Cap de Creus peninsula with the most extraordinary coastal town in Catalonia: Cadaqués. At the northern end of the Costa Brava, Cadaqués has survived as a town that has retained the captivating charms of a fishing village in a breathtakingly beautiful setting and attracted painters and artists for more than a century. It looks the same as it did many years ago, and could be described as Catalonia's Capri. Cadaqués is difficult to reach by road and this has preserved it from mass tourism. Many artists, particularly painters and sculptors, have their homes and studios in the town. Some of Ferran Adrià's protégés have moved here and set up restaurants and cocktail bars of amazing quality. Cadaqués doesn't have much beach, but it does have pretty little coves. Around it we find Cap de Creus, which you can't afford to miss with its beautiful twisted, jagged rocks. Picasso fell in love with the area. However, it was Salvador Dalí (Figueres, 1904-1989) who linked his entire artistic career to Cadaqués and brought it to worldwide attention. Everything in Dalí's works, particularly his most famous, most surrealist, paintings, is imbued with the spirit of Cadaqués and its environs. He made his home in a fisherman's hut in the neighbouring cove of Portlligat. Dalí and his wife Gala (a Russian exile who had previously been married to the French surrealist poet Paul Éluard) extended the house to their own tastes, with their highly personal design and the greatest respect for the surrounding area. The result is an absolute must for visitors wishing to gain an insight into the world of Dalí and Gala and to see the interaction between nature, culture and the creation of art. Dalí, who opposed the popular-frontist and communist drift of the surrealist movement during the 1930s, ended up creating a magical dwelling which most closely resembles Pablo Neruda's house on Isla Negra in Chile. What a paradox! The anti-communist and communist had in common tastes, hobbies, collections and aesthetic values, and a love of the solitary life, with their much loved spouses, by the sea surrounded by rocks. There is also another detail that binds them together: they were born in the same year, 1904. This reminds us of the fact that, as the years go by, being contemporaries brings you closer together than sharing ideologie. Isla Negra and Portlligat are two places you have to visit in order to understand the aesthetic universe of the decades of the middle of the 20th century.

Cadaqués encapsulates, and is the greatest exponent of the Costa Brava: sea and stone in constant tension, making and unmaking form and light. It is now a peaceful spot where you'll find the good life. From Cadaqués — or going towards Cadaqués — you can enjoy the landscapes and coves of the Costa Brava, the wonderful villages on the coast and in the Alt Empordà and Baix Empordà, the Dalí Museum in Figueres, and the captivating city of Girona. On the Costa Brava, and especially the strip running from Blanes to Begur, highlights include Tossa de Mar, Sant Feliu de Guíxols, S'Agaró, Palamós and Calella de Palafrugell. Each one of these towns combines great beaches and coves with their own individual and unique charm, with well-preserved urban spaces, some of them medieval and others more recent. They all offer a plethora of dining options and terraces with amazing views. A little further up, in the Gulf of Roses next door to L'Escala, you'll find the ruins of Empúries, the archaeological remains that provide evidence of Greek settlers in Catalonia and are located in a magnificent natural setting. They stand near Sant Martí d'Empúries, a delightful corner of the coast, with views over the beaches, coves, pine glades and little villages that still captivate visitors from abroad as they must have captivated the colonisers almost 3,000 years ago. Not far from Empúries, in the inland area of the Baix Empordà, you'll find the best example of an Iberian settlement in Catalonia: Ullastret.

In the inland area of the Baix Empordà — known as Empordanet — there is an endless list of unmissable villages. It is an area with a very high standard of living, with micro landscapes, tucked-away spots, and exclusive farmhouses, or *masias*, many of them transformed into high-end hotels and restaurants. Empordanet attracts tourists from around the world and, of course, countless visitors from Barcelona and Madrid. Today it is a small world that serves as a privileged refuge for the Catalan elites, from right- and left-wing intellectuals to successful businesspeople and politicians. The counties of Girona offer the most diverse array of landscapes. The beaches and coves are just a short distance away from the mountains and ski slopes, gently rolling plains, beautifully preserved villages, quiet minor roads, green ways for cycling and secluded golf courses. Girona, a beautifully preserved city, is the centre of this happy universe. It is currently the best Catalan city in terms of standard of living, with a vibrant university and cultural life and appealing shops. In the space of a generation it has brought to the fore the beautiful architectural features that have lain hidden. The perfect location for films on a medieval theme, every corner of the city centre amazes those who explore it.

The painstakingly restored medieval Jewish Quarter is truly stunning.

From Cap de Creus to the Vall d'Aran

(via Andorra)

The north-western tip of the Catalan triangle is quite different. The southern side of the geographical area of the Vall d'Aran abuts onto the Vall de Boí, a place steeped in symbolism with rivers that flow out into the Mediterranean. Nestling in the Pyrenees, the Vall de Boí is a UNESCO World Heritage Site. Cadaqués and Cap de Creus stand at the eastern end of the Pyrenees in the Alberes mountains which plunge steeply down to the sea. The Vall de Boí stands right in the middle of the Pyrenees. Just like all the areas in the great Catalan mountain range, it would have been more heavily populated 1,000 years ago than it is today. At the time it was a place of safety, its natural surroundings and distance from the sea and navigable rivers protecting it from invaders. This greater safety, together with a relatively warm climate that was widespread in Europe during the centuries immediately before and after the year 1,000 AD, made it ideal for agriculture. The valley had lush pastures for livestock, and a great many villages were built in the area. The abundance of churches and chapels provides ample proof of the density of the population. In the Vall de Boí there are more churches than the current number of inhabitants require. This means that the population must have been much higher a thousand years ago in a place that came to be known as one of the cradles of Catalan civilisation.

Many areas claim the title "cradle of Catalan civilisation" and there's no doubt they are all worthy of it in some way: whether it's due to their ancient churches and convents, the aristocratic dynasties that originated there, or their pioneering role in building the Catalonia of the Counts, or any other reason. The Vall de Boí, at the north-western tip of Catalonia, is a cradle of Catalan civilisation because it was so densely populated and the focus of the Christian conquest of the Ebro valley.

Indeed, the barons of Erill la Vall were very astute and helped King Alfonso of Aragon (and Count of Barcelona) in his expeditions to conquer Zaragoza and the Ebro valley, The baron of Erill la Vall was richly rewarded. He invested his wealth in embellishing the churches in the Vall de Boí. He hired church builders, fresco painters, sculptors of statues and craftsmen with a wide range of skills to provide his valley with landmarks that would make him famous and be a source of pride to his vassals. The result was a surprisingly dense grouping of Romanesque churches in the Lombard style, with tall, slender bell towers. The church interiors were decorated with elegantly executed wall frescoes (or murals on wood) in vibrant colours. The whole ensemble must have looked truly stunning at the time and committed the baronetcy of Erill la Vall to expanding and preserving its artistic and architectural leadership.

The inhabitants of the valley must have taken part in countless operations to conquer and settle the lands in the Ebro valley, from Lleida to Zaragoza. The area came to be known as "la franja", the strip of territory that forms the boundary between Aragon and Catalonia. Catalan was the common language because, despite being under the jurisdiction of the king of Aragon, the area was in the diocese of Lleida. This situation continued, with total normality, for hundreds of years. However, in the 20th century, it became a bête noire for those seeking Spanish unity who were determined to eradicate all traces of Catalan on "la franja", the "non" boundary between Catalonia and Aragon.

Anyone visiting the Vall de Boí today — and we strongly recommend you do — will find a veritable treasure trove that has lost none of the beauty it had a thousand years ago. The artistic treasures of the valley's churches, which fell into a state of disrepair as people left to live elsewhere, were rediscovered by Catalan institutions in the early 20th century. The expeditions led by the architects Puig i Cadafalch and Domènech i Montaner identified and catalogued the valley's heritage and drew up a preservation policy which involved moving frescoes and works of art to episcopal and national museums in Catalonia. The Museu Nacional d'Art de Catalunya, in Barcelona, is home to many of these works of art, but you'll also find them beautifully showcased at the episcopal museums in Vic, Solsona, the Seu d'Urgell and Lleida.

The new political and cultural awareness has made it possible to admire the treasures of the valley in situ, through copies or virtual reconstructions, such as the innovative video mapping projection recreating the frescoes inside the church of Sant Climent de Taüll.

What we have said about the Vall de Boí also applies to the other valleys in the Pyrenees, from the neighbouring Vall d'Aran to the far-away Vall de Camprodon, in the area of Girona. The entire Pyrenean mountain range is the cradle of Catalan civilisation and preserves the most genuine expressions of the new Christian society that emerged from the ruins of the Roman province with its capital in *Tarraco*, present-day Tarragona.

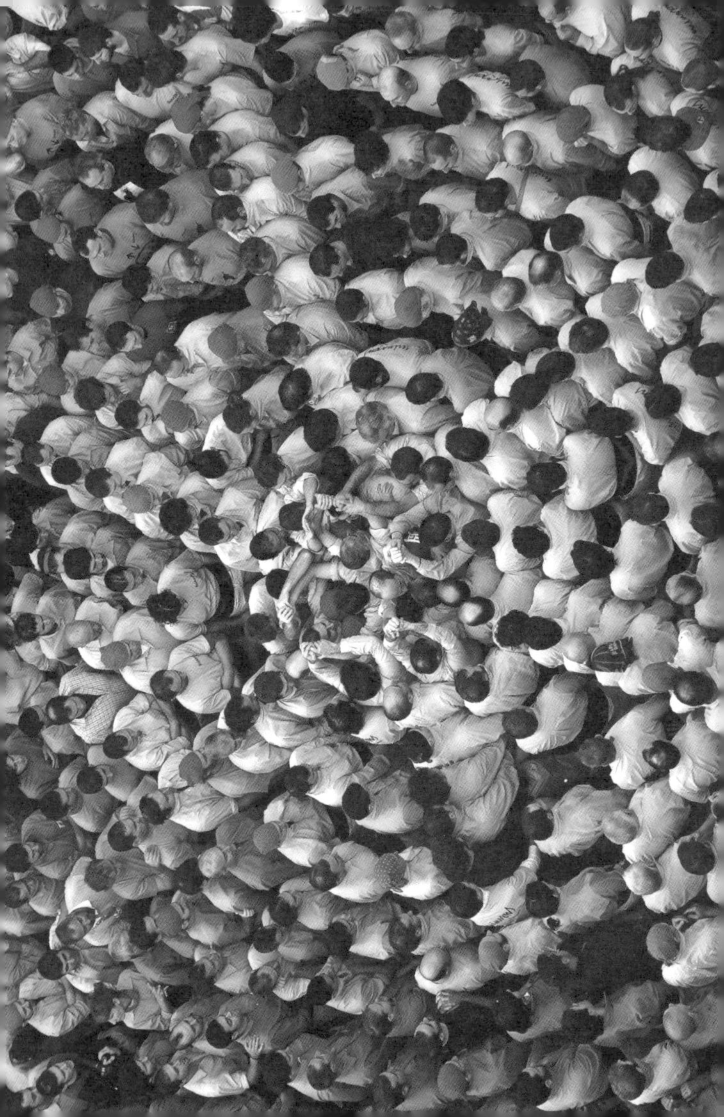

What are Catalans like?

First impressions

The tourists who visit Catalonia already have a number of pre-conceived impressions about Catalans. They are gathered in the surveys performed by local bodies keen to improve the image of the region. Let's go through them, starting with the one that crops up most frequently.

Catalans keep to a strange timetable, particularly when they eat and turn in for the night. Although they have breakfast at more or less the same time as other countries, they have lunch quite a bit later, and dinner much later than their visitors usually do. The most striking difference is the time they go to bed. We might say that Catalans delay their activities in comparison with other countries. The people in the other Mediterranean regions of Spain are the only ones who come close. There are two reasons for the idiosyncratic Catalan timetable. Firstly, Catalonia isn't in the right time zone if we consider its actual geographical location. Before the Second World War, Spain was on GMT whereas now it is an hour ahead. Secondly, the warm climate and long daylight hours are the perfect combination for spending time in the open air, meaning people spend more time outdoors and go to bed late. Catalans have gradually adapted to their visitors' habits and tastes while visitors have fully embraced theirs. Catalans go to the beach in summer, even on weekdays; they love whiling away the time at a pavement café, having a coffee in the morning and a drink in the evening; they love *a la fresca* dining and going out at night. If the truth were told, they would much rather enjoy the "summer" timetable, which is two hours ahead of GMT, all the year round.

Catalans work long hours and their working days are divided up by long breaks. Those in favour of rationalising working hours and achieving the right work-life balance despair of the situation, but the facts speak for themselves: on average, Catalans work a lot of hours and sleep very little. Studies show this clearly: they sleep at least one hour less than northern Europeans do.

There was a time when Catalan cuisine was of good quality but rather uninteresting. The latest generation of chefs has brought about a spectacular turn around, and the same is true for all those products associated with eating well: wines, olive oils, bread, cakes. Fine dining has triumphed and the Catalans couldn't be prouder. Not only are they enthusiastic consumers but great evangelists too.

Like the French and the Italians — who are the masters — it could be said that Catalans enjoy drinking in moderation, not in excess. They don't quite match the Italians, who don't have an actual word for hangover, but they're not far behind.

Catalans are much noisier than almost all the tourists who visit them. There is much greater tolerance of loud noises in public spaces and this comes as a surprise to visitors. The situation is changing, but there's still a long way to go before we improve it completely. Bars and restaurants are much noisier than the ones in more northerly countries. However, the noise won't seem so bad if you have been in the south or west of Spain before you arrive in Catalonia.

Standards in the way Catalans dress have fallen in recent years. They dress differently to other Spaniards and, if the truth were told, much worse than the Italians. This is probably due to the proliferation of shops selling clothes at low prices. The tendency to dress more casually with undefined, darker, sludgy brown colours has become widespread. In fact, the Catalans have an expression for this particular shade, "color de gos com fuig", which translates as "dog running away colour". Catalonia tends to be ahead of the curve in Spain, and this can be attributed to the effects of globalisation that Catalonia had embraced before the rest of the country.

Clean or dirty? It's really difficult to voice and opinion about this fundamental aspect of any society. But it's really important! The quick, and correct, answer is that the Catalans, and Mediterraneans as a whole are much cleaner in their homes than they are in public spaces. This means that there's still a lot of room for improvement, particularly when it comes to the cleanliness of the toilets in public amenities. When you cross into Catalonia via the motorway from France, people are really disappointed with the toilets at the service areas. Fortunately, now that Catalan society is catering more to tourists, this has led to greater supervision of these areas than there was previously. The authorities and governments now take these aspects into account when issuing and renewing permits.

Beyond the most obvious aspects, how can we define the Catalans' character?

Serious or fun? Catalans have a reputation throughout Spain as a serious, not to say boring, bunch. Quite the opposite to the Andalusians, who are always being funny and cracking jokes. One of the merits many people found in José Montilla — the president of the Catalan government from 2006 to 2010, who hailed from Cordoba but had moved to Catalonia in his youth — was that he seemed totally Catalan because he was so serious and "bland".

Generous or stingy? Catalans used to have a reputation throughout Spain as a tight-fisted people who didn't give anything away. There is a grain of truth in this because it reflects a community who had scant natural resources and had to earn a living through trade, while being subjected to the vagaries of the markets. In recent years, prosperity has turned around this clichéd image, which had earned the Catalans a number of pejorative and politically incorrect nicknames

Trustworthy or untrustworthy? Conversely, Catalans have had, and have a reputation as responsible people who always keep their word. For a region that has grown as a result of private enterprise, these were key virtues in order to survive and prosper. They still are, although maybe less so than before, but they remain a valid simplification of the average Catalan.

Religious or non-believers? Catalan society has been, and remains, Catholic, but it was certainly the first society on the Iberian Peninsula to become secular and to distance itself the most from religious practices, regardless of their ideological persuasion. Nowadays, Catholicism is the majority religion among those who express some kind of religious convictions. However, it now faces stiff competition from the new religions associated with the mass immigration from 1996 to 2008, from the non-Catholic, Christian world, or the Muslim community.

Straight or gay? Catalan society has always been far ahead in its recognition and acceptance of people of different sexual orientations. The Spanish government legalised same-sex marriages in 2005 and the change has gradually permeated all areas of life. It has now become commonplace in the programmes of political parties and at all levels of government. The result is absolute respect for people of different sexual persuasions, and the recognition by society of all kinds of couples without any risk of exclusion. The emergence and success of many places where the LGTBI community are made to feel welcome have had a visible impact on tourism.

How are Catalans changing? Just like people in the rest of the western world, Catalans are changing their traditional patterns of behaviour. Families have few children and they are often lone-parent, or same-sex families. Many families have become more complex as a result of divorces, remarriages and parents getting back together. At the same time, a new generation of Catalans has appeared: the children of immigrants, who live very different lifestyles. Their integration and contact with the local population is creating widespread diversification in the Catalan identity.

Gregarious and individualistic

The crowds that descend on the Barça stadium suggest that Catalans are an outgoing people. The same can be said for the demonstrations that attract millions of people in the defence of a number of causes, from the protests against the Iraq War and the terrorist attacks by ETA and the jihadis in Catalonia, to those welcoming exiles from the war in Syria. Particularly noteworthy are the demonstrations defending Catalonia's right to self-government and independence, together with those standing up for the unity of Spain, those calling for the freedom of political prisoners, and the spectacular gatherings that have taken place every 11th September — Catalonia's National Day — since 2012. Catalans feel at ease demonstrating. To them it's a form of shared political expression and respect for their civic and community conscience.

Catalan society is highly individualistic. This is arguably its most distinctive feature, the source of its energy and the cause of its weakness. The

Catalans' individualism explains their creativity, vitality and dynamism, as well as their all-consuming jealousy, misgivings at other people's successes, and strong dislike of gregariousness. The fact that they enjoy going on massive demonstrations so much, is, indeed, extraordinary. It could be said that the Catalans' restraint and self-control are the natural result of their aversion to expressing their feelings in public. When Catalans go on demonstrations, they don't make any noise on the way there; they only begin to chant or shout when they reach the place where the demonstration has been convened. The fact remains that they are much better suited to stand-alone activities. But this can trigger inherent limitations when devising large-scale joint business projects. It is said that the origins of Catalan individualism are geographical in nature: in Catalonia there are no vast, sweeping landscapes; everything is small and varied. There isn't one climate that affects all the Catalans in the same way. The climate can change within a relatively small distance. This means that the opportunities to join together to mark happy or sad occasions are fairly rare. A sense of solidarity or collective identity represents a conscious effort to correct the tendency towards individualism.

The Catalans' great fondness for mushroom-hunting is another example of the finely tuned balance between gregariousness and individualism. Catalans love eating wild mushrooms and theirs is a large consumer market. The best time for picking mushrooms is early autumn, when the kitchens in people's homes, and restaurants too, set about preparing and eating mushrooms. When the weather conditions are right, Catalans head out en masse to hunt for mushrooms. You'll find tailbacks at 5am on the road from Barcelona to the mountains, 100 kilometres to the north. The aim is for all of them, in their vast numbers, to get there by daybreak. Yet, what they are actually doing represents the height of their individualism: they'll seek out deserted corners of the forest where nobody is around and they can find their highly prized mushrooms. The hordes of Catalan mushroom-hunters represent the infinite sum of individualities in search of their piece of woodland. If they find anything promising, they won't tell anybody except, perhaps, their husbands or wives, and even they are competitive with each other! The haul of mushrooms, lovingly displayed in specially made wicker baskets, is a symbol of success and source of pride for the pickers, who fill them to the brim, and a sign of failure for those who come away empty handed. Mushroom-hunting is individualism in action. Nobody will let on where they have been or where they have found the mushrooms they are carrying. And everyone will be pleased with their achievements, no matter how small.

This mindset won't conquer America or build an empire, or create businesses on a par with Coca-Cola or Siemens. Let's be under no illusion, Catalans are charming because they aren't overbearing or obsessive. They embrace difference with delight, and love exploring small worlds, collecting obscure objects, dreaming about impossible utopias. You'll find them making films, immersed in artistic and literary creativity, reinventing exquisite dishes, setting up new and exclusive wineries...

Few leading members of the military have been born in Catalonia. However, it is the birthplace of large numbers of clerical and lay missionaries, from the church or with communist leanings. This is another manifestation of Catalan individualism associated with a widespread character trait: generosity. In the land of the so-called "tight-fisted" people, generous ones abound. They are generous with their lives and money. The surprising thing is, when faced with individual and collective misfortunes, or in the pursuit of research into finding cures for illnesses, vast numbers of Catalans give blood, donate organs and money, as well as food for the most disadvantaged members of society, wherever they may be. Equally surprising is the number of families who have a member taking part in missions or cooperative development projects to help people in the poorest parts of the world, where people who have been educated in Catalonia offer their skills and know-how to those less fortunate than themselves. You'll often come across people who have dedicated their entire lives to business and decide to devote themselves to helping others when they retire.

'Seny i rauxa'. Common sense or impulsiveness

Classic essays on Catalans in Spain have established two concepts that embody the Catalan character: 'seny' and 'rauxa' (the former could be loosely translated as 'common sense' and the latter as 'impulsiveness'). 'Seny' describes a rational, reasonable attitude, that avoids conflicts and problems, and always looks for solutions. Catalans are level headed and have common sense. This natural state usually prevails and has made it possible for Catalans to trade, sell and attract people, while being responsible and trustworthy. To a large extent, this leads Catalans to make pacts (another cliché about them) be they political, business, social or intellectual.

However, from time to time, Catalans set their commonsense aside and let impulsiveness, or 'rauxa' take over. 'Rauxa' is defined by risky decisions, immediate reactions, questioning everything, breaking with convention, revolution. Throughout their history, the impulsiveness of the Catalans has led to several wars to secede from the Spanish Crown as well as a number of declarations of independence, uprisings and revolts. Based on this interpretation, the current push for independence could be seen as another episode of 'rauxa' which is awaiting an injection of 'seny'.

Ideology and identity

To avoid oversimplifying Catalonia and Catalans as a place and people that join together with one voice, we should remember that one of their predominant traits is an ability to fall out with each other for any reason. Their internal divisions ultimately account for the fact that they don't have their own state and belong to a country that has been able to prioritise, at crucial times, its own unity above and beyond all other differences. Conversely, the Catalans have ended up prioritising their differences. There are two types: those related to ideology and those related to identity. The ideological ones reflect — as they do around the world — the customary differences between the left and right and can be very intense and passionate. Those related to identity reflect different feelings of belonging and are central to opinion surveys which always ask their sample group if they feel only Catalan, only Spanish, more Catalan than Spanish, more Spanish than Catalan, or as Catalan as they do Spanish.

Feelings and celebrations

The feelings of Catalans are widely reflected in two major celebrations that everyone joins in. Whenever the Catalans have managed to reclaim some degree of self-government they have been quite clear about the date they want to hold their national festival: 11th September. On this day, the Catalans remember that they were once a nation with a state and choose to commemorate a defeat rather than a victory. On 11th September 1714, Barcelona surrendered to the troops of Philip V, the first king of the House of Bourbon. But Catalan society also wanted to have an alternative celebration that sought to convey the values of Catalan identity and culture: Sant Jordi (Saint George), on 23rd April. This is reflected by the fact that Jordi is the most popular Catalan boys' name. Catalonia shares its devotion to Sant Jordi with England, Greece, Russia, Georgia, Bulgaria and Portugal and the neighbouring region of Aragon. In 1926, the day of Sant Jordi — which falls on the same day Cervantes died — was made official book day in Spain. Booksellers set up their stalls in the streets and sold their books at discounted prices. The tradition of giving a book became widespread and was soon associated with the long-established tradition of giving a rose (Sant Jordi is the Catalan equivalent of Valentine's Day). Initially, men would give roses to their loved ones (starting with their mothers), and women would give books to men (as the years have gone by, people have bought and given books without distinguishing between the sexes). The initiative to combine selling books and roses was an immediate success and soon became a much-loved tradition. It is now the most wonderful day enjoyed by Catalans, particularly when it falls on a weekday and the weather is fine.

Catalan, the secret of the Catalans

Catalan is the Catalans' own language. It isn't the only one; they also speak Spanish, the official language of Spain. In fact, Spanish is the most widely spoken. It hasn't been easy for Catalan to survive up to the present day and have a future of its own. It has been a minority language inside a state with a strong language that is universal in scope: Spanish. In France, the numbers of people who speak Catalan has dwindled. In Spain, the language has survived and remains an energetic force. We can say, with all certainty, that the success of Catalan represents the other side of the failure of Spanish to take over completely. Be that as it may, today's Catalans speak Catalan because schools guarantee the teaching of both Spanish and Catalan. Catalan is spoken because families have preserved and cultivated it as their language. For centuries, Catalans have been aware that they couldn't impose their language and adopted a bilingualism that has become second nature. This means they can switch from Catalan to Spanish depending on who they are talking to, and even in smaller circles of friends, to work colleagues, family members, their husband, wife and any permutations of new and old acquaintances. They choose the language according the person they are talking to. They get no thanks for it, despite the fact that it is a highly sophisticated cultural skill. This has resulted in a growth in Spanish, whose speakers never change language, to the detriment of Catalan which could experience a decrease in the number of speakers due to a simple network effect. Catalan hasn't declined because of the social prestige it enjoys, in spite of the small obstacles that have been put in its way.

This means that Catalans particularly enjoy those occasions when they can switch to speaking Catalan, because it gives them respite, and takes them to a comfortable, friendly, understanding place. This is, of course, true when they are away from home, but it is also the case anywhere in Catalonia. There are many places where Spanish is the dominant language, either for simple sociological reasons, and, more often than not, for political ones. This is because there are buildings run by central government where Spanish is more widely spoken, for instance, the law courts and police stations. If Catalan speakers can use Catalan in places that are usually hostile to the language, the sense of relief is immediate. More often than not, the opposite is true.

Visitors to Catalonia should be aware that Catalans really love their language. Any sign of respect and empathy for Catalan will be greatly appreciated. Speaking the Catalans' language is the greatest gift a foreigner can give them.

Indeed, the Pyrenees stretch from the north-eastern to the north-western ends of Catalonia, marking the border with France. The border between Spain and France was decided in the Treaty of the Pyrenees of 1659 when the king of Castile and Aragon, and king of Spain, Philip IV, who was from the House of Hapsburg, and the king of France, Louis XIV, made peace, bringing to an end almost 20 years of attempts by the Catalans to become independent from their king. In the treaty, Catalonia lost all its territories in Roussillon, Perpignan and even the castle-fortress of Salses, which stood at the northernmost end of the Principality of Catalonia.

The small valley of Andorra managed to come out of these negotiations as an independent state and the only one where Catalan is the official language. Andorra is something of an anomaly, like Lichtenstein. It has survived as a fiercely independent valley between two states with a long-standing tradition. Andorra raises the profile of the Pyrenees around the world and lends it an identity. Co-governed by the president of France and the bishop of the Seu d'Urgell, it is a tiny democracy that, until recently, enjoyed special tax exemptions. The European Union and the United States are exerting more and more pressure to bring its banks into line with the rest of the world. Be that as it may, there are many other reasons to visit. Andorra attracts tourists from around the world, who don't only come here to ski, but enjoy browsing the shops and a spot of retail therapy. For Catalonia, Andorra has always represented a dream of freedom and been the gateway which brought in new goods from Europe during the bleakest years of the Franco regime.

The Catalan Pyrenees are the sunny side of the mountain range, while the French Pyrenees are the shady side. The Catalan Pyrenees are drier and rockier, while the French Pyrenees are greener and more wooded. Nevertheless, the Catalan Pyrenees provide a breathtaking expanse of nature and could be termed the Catalan outback. The geography of Catalonia is defined by the pre-Pyrenean ridge and the pre-coastal mountain range. In the broadest sense, the Pyrenees include the pre-Pyrenean ridge. They are wild, inhospitable lands, that have always had Carlist sympathies, where the peasants achieved early emancipation because the feudal lords could only obtain poor yields from the unfertile soil. They are the spaces of the vast natural parks in the mountains, of ecclesiastical towns like the Seu d'Urgell, Solsona, and, to some extent, Vic, and the commercial and industrial towns of Berga and Olot. They are all beautiful, well preserved and wealthy and have excellent museums. These lands are popular with hikers and espouse a culture of respect and care for the environment.

From the Vall de Boí to the Ebro Delta

The central massif and central depression lie to the south of the Pyrenees and the pre-Pyrenean ridge. They lie within the region known as the Terres de Lleida, with the capital, Lleida, standing proudly in the centre. The city enjoyed a period of splendour in medieval times — when it was the seat of a major university — and in the modern era, until it was razed to the ground for providing a gateway to Catalonia, a land that always wanted to be different from Castile. Now restored to its former glory, the city retains two iconic landmarks that reflect its splendid past: the cathedral, the Seu Vella, and the Museu Episcopal. The ruins of the Seu Vella are an imposing sight. Perched on the hill that has been a symbol of Lleida since the time of the first human settlers, it towers over the plateau known as the Plana de Ponent. The Seu is an impressive building. It is gradually being restored and always leaves a strong impression on the minds of its visitors. Lleida lost its university and many other things, but it has successfully built new premises for its wonderful diocesan and county museum, the Museu de Lleida.

Heading south-west, both sides of the Catalan triangle begin to narrow. Here you'll find the city of Tortosa and an extraordinary geographical feature: the Ebro Delta. The Terres de l'Ebre, or Baix Ebre, show a different side to Catalonia which is nonetheless reminiscent of other areas of the region.

There are few deltas in the Mediterranean because there are few great rivers with a high volume of water that flows out into this great ocean. The Ebro is one of them. The Rhone and the Po are the other two on the northern shore. The Danube Delta lies in the Black Sea, like a number of Russian rivers. On the southern shore, we find the Nile. None of them have deltas that have altered the coastline as much as the Ebro has.

The Ebro Delta has been formed over time. Medieval and modern maps show how its shape has changed in order to expand. It hasn't continued to grow at the same rate as it did over the last thousand years because the construction of large hydroelectric dams throughout the Ebro basin, and its major tributaries, has reduced the amount of alluvial deposits. The political conflict that has pitted the inhabitants of the Ebro Delta, and the inhabitants of the Baix Ebre as a whole, against the people from south-east Spain, Murcia and Andalusia, is their opposition to the transfer of water from the Ebro to the southern basins of the Mediterranean. The people from the Baix Ebre are afraid they'll lose water and alluvial deposits and the delta will shrink.

The delta has created almost 400 square kilometres of extremely fertile farmland. It wasn't like this at the beginning. The land was boggy and unsanitary. However, from the 18th century onwards, people began investing in irrigation channels that helped desalinate the delta and make its potential as farmland a reality. From the 18th to 20th centuries, the delta was transformed from a very poor area to a prosperous one. The investors who made a commitment to the delta's agricultural future came out winning. Today the delta is a major rice-growing area, and its produce is in great demand on domestic and European markets. It also produces top-quality fruit and vegetables and is one of southern Europe's most interesting refuges for wildlife, particularly bird species.

The stabilisation of the coastline, which had shifted back and forth for centuries, has brought a new source of wealth that remains untapped: beaches. The ones that already existed used to change place and shape every year. They escaped the tourist invasion of the 1960s and managed to avoid the hordes of visitors from the early 21st century. Slowly but surely, the beaches have become more permanent. The local authorities have declared nearly all of them protected conservation areas making it impossible for any building to take place. Demands from the community have led to improvements in the services at some beaches. The result: 40 kilometres of wild, unspoilt beautiful beaches, that never get crowded and are perfect for outdoor pursuits. Trabucador, Fangar, and Marquesa beaches, and a few others, are an extraordinary coastal reserve. They should be protected even more and are worthy of our unremitting admiration. They are a combination of Antillean beaches (in the areas facing the continent) and Atlantic beaches (in the areas facing the sea), with clean, peaceful waters, that can become choppy due to the wind, yet are sheltered, and have an abundance of fish.

The Baix Ebre isn't just home to the mouth of the Ebro and its delta. It also has Tortosa as its capital. Tortosa has always been a city, like Lleida, Barcelona and Tarragona. They are all cities built in amazing natural settings. Lleida perches on a hilltop that towers above the Plain of Lleida and marks the border between Catalonia and Aragon. Barcelona stands on a low hill inside a natural harbour and Tarragona is similar. The equivalent town in the northern Empordà didn't prosper: Empúries was unable to become the *Tarraco* of the north. Girona took its place. Tortosa grew and stood for centuries on a hill that kept watch over the lower course of the Ebro, a channel that could be navigated using technology that preceded steamboats. Its central geographical location made it a natural departure point for the entire Vall de l'Ebre, and easily connected Catalonia with the parts of Spain beyond the Ebro. It has always been a capital, although it lost its status as provincial capital. Tortosa has given rise to monumental buildings: a castle, cathedral, palaces, schools, churches and monasteries, a commodities exchange, an abattoir and bridges. Tortosa is home to the only important ensemble of Renaissance architecture in Catalonia, which shows that Castile, rather than Catalonia, was its economic powerhouse. At the same time, it is the capital of the counties where Catalan is most widely spoken. Newly restored, Tortosa has wonderful surprises in store for its visitors. Its natural surroundings remind us that southern Catalonia was under Muslim occupation until the early 12th century, and that the climate and landscape of the Valencian Region begins in the Terres de l'Ebre: orchards, gardens and irrigation farming, a love of fine food and wine, and keeping cool, which is indispensable in warm countries. If you want to enjoy wonderful views of the area, climb to the top of Mont Caro, right next to Tortosa. Standing 1,447 metres above sea level it overlooks the entire Terres de l'Ebre and, on a clear day, you can see as far as the Pyrenees and Mallorca. Forty-four kilometres further up the Ebro,

Miravet Castle is a strategic point which controlled the river for more than a millennium. It was the fortress that had always kept watch over the place where the Ebro ceases to gently wind its way through fertile land and cuts through a narrow neck of land before widening just before Tortosa and making its way to the sea. The fortress was first occupied by the Moors and then by the Knights Templar. It later became famous as the place where the blueprint for the Autonomy Statute of Catalonia was drawn up in 2006.

The neighbouring counties of Aragon and the Valencian Region stretch beyond Miravet to the west of the Ebro. They are overlooked by the mountain ridge of Els Ports which has Mont Caro as its highest point. Els Ports form a natural boundary between the three continental divisions of the old Kingdom of Aragon. To the north of Els Ports lies the village of Horta de Sant Joan, where Picasso and his girlfriend, Fernande Olivier, spent long periods of time in their youth and where he painted his first cubist oils.

Inland Catalonia

Further exploration of the Catalan triangle wouldn't be possible without mentioning the most extraordinary place inside its perimeter: Montserrat. To use a geometric metaphor, it is Catalonia's physical and spiritual centre of mass.

Indeed, the massif of Montserrat and its monastery are Catalonia's centre of gravity while the monastery is, at the same time, its undeniable spiritual centre. The unusual shape of the massif — which is jagged like the teeth of a saw — has attracted visitors to Catalonia since time immemorial. Nestling among the mountain's peaks, the monastery is a place of pilgrimage and a popular visitor attraction. It guards the statue of the Black Madonna, or Our Lady of Montserrat, which has given us the most popular Catalan woman's name: Montserrat. The monastery is a symbol of Catalan identity and integration for newcomers to the region. All the political parties recognise its symbolic importance and readily pay it homage and provide it with financial and governmental support. The monastery was destroyed during the Peninsular War, (1808-1814) and the Third Carlist War (1872-1876) and its architecture is deliberately Historicist in style to remind us of its ancient heritage. Following the damage suffered in 1874, the Catalan affluent classes generously and enthusiastically funded its swift reconstruction.

Montserrat is a religious destination, as well as a cultural one in the strictest sense of the word (it is home to a great museum and an extraordinary library) and in the broadest sense too (concerts by the boys' choir, the Escolania, and mass being sung). It has many hiking trails that lead to viewing spots with breathtaking vistas and the foot sheer drops that challenge the most experienced climbers. On public holidays it is packed with tourists, hikers and walkers. It never disappoints because it offers each and every visitor something spiritual and material (including the excellent produce of the land).

Montserrat is the great iconic landmark in the centre of Catalonia but there are other monasteries in the region that have earned a place in the national consciousness as well as being religious symbols. We find the great monasteries of Poblet and Santes Creus in what came to be known as New Catalonia following the Christian Reconquest from the Moors after 1100 AD, as well as the less well-known Vallbona de les Monges, which is home to a community of nuns. They were also the burial sites of the kings and queens of Aragon. The monasteries were lavishly built in the Gothic style and have been faithfully restored after many years of neglect. They played a vital role in the resettlement of the reconquered lands. Poblet now houses a historic archive. The great monastery of Sant Pere de Rodes stands to the north, near El Port de la Selva and a short distance from Cadaqués. The monastery of Ripoll, which was equally important, is now used as a church, making us forget that it was once a great monastery. Not far from Ripoll we find Sant Joan de les Abadesses, which was home to a community of nuns. All the monasteries in the north are Romanesque while those in the south are Gothic. Near Solsona, we find a real oddity, the monastery of El Miracle, a Renaissance-style building with a spectacular baroque altar which is arguably the biggest and best preserved in Catalonia. To the south, we find another unusual building, the Carthusian priory of Scala Dei, from which the region, known as Priorat, takes its name. The priory was destroyed following the disentailment of the church's property, and has now been painstakingly rebuilt and restored, offering a wonderful insight into the way monasteries became top-flight places of political, intellectual and entrepreneurial endeavour. The priory of Scala Dei nestles in the foothills of the Montsant ridge, which is the one that most closely resembles Montserrat. Nearby, perched on an inaccessible hilltop, stands the village of Siurana, the last redoubt of Moorish rule in medieval Catalonia. It gave birth to the legend of the Leap of the Moorish Queen who jumped off the precipice on her horse to avoid being captured by her enemies. It is said that horseshoe marks can still be seen etched into the stone as the animal tried to break its fall. Siurana is breathtakingly beautiful and a constant reminder of the countless magical places to be found in the many Catalonias described in our book. Diversity in diversity.

Catalans — whether they are believers or not — are particularly fond of the monastery trail, and the same is true of Christian visitors to Catalonia. The trail provides a wonderful overview of the region as the monasteries are always located in beautiful settings and have been designed to ambitious aesthetic specifications. Shrines are another series of religious buildings which are more inaccessible but placed in spectacular locations, particularly the numerous ones perched on hilltops. You can take a fascinating tour of Catalonia and visit some of these shrines. They include Mare de Déu del Mont, which overlooks Mount Canigó and commands views of all the Alt Empordà; Mare de Déu de Queralt, which overlooks Berguedà; Mare de Déu de Bellmunt and Mare de Déu de Cabrera, which rise above the Plain of Vic; Sant Llorenç del Munt, which is the finest viewing spot on the massif of Montserrat; and Mare de Déu del Far, which, despite being located right in the middle of the Girona region stands so high above the valley that it can be seen from the sea, just like a lighthouse ('far' in Catalan). Many of them have restaurants and hotels attached and provide memorable experiences due to their spectacular views.

Cardona, and its castle in particular, form a second centre of mass, but this time a military rather than spiritual one. A little further up from Montserrat, heading north along the river Cardener, a tributary of the Llobregat, we find Cardona and its famous salt mines. More recently it has begun to be better known for its castle and collegiate church. The castle, which was built to defend the border between Old (Christian) Catalonia and Moorish Catalonia (which was renamed New Catalonia when it was recaptured by the Christians), was the last Catalan stronghold during the War of the Spanish Succession. Cardona Castle only surrendered to its attackers when it received orders to do so from Barcelona, which fell on 11th September 1714. It is also famous as the main location for Orson Welles' Shakespearian masterpiece, *Chimes at Midnight*.

Speaking of castles, and you'll find them all over Catalonia, it's important to remember that, despite tensions running high and their profound distrust of one another, Catalonia and Castile have one thing that binds them closely together:

their name. Some experts believe that Catalonia and Castile are toponyms that mean the same thing etymologically: land of castles or 'castelani'. Two toponyms that are as close semantically as they are divided historically.

In addition to monasteries, shrines and castles, the geographical centre of Catalonia has a plethora of small towns and villages that are well worth a visit. Manresa, next to Montserrat, has a splendid cathedral. Further east, Vic has the most famous main square in Catalonia, which still holds a wonderful weekly market every Saturday, and has a recently built, beautiful episcopal museum which houses a fabulous collection of Romanesque paintings and sculptures. Further west, lies Solsona, another bishopric, like Vic, but smaller, with a perfectly preserved old town with a world-class cathedral and episcopal museum.

Some of the small inland towns are prefixed by the word 'caldes' (thermal springs in Catalan): Caldes de Malavella, Caldes de Montbui, and Caldes de Boí. These thermal springs were well known to the Roman settlers and provide proof of how far their empire had spread in Catalonia. There is also a spa town on the Maresme coast, Caldes d'Estrac.

During your exploration of the inland counties of Catalonia, particularly those on the pre-coastal area, as well as some areas of the coast, you will have realised that the undulating landscape of the vineyards reminds us that the culture of wine and 'cava' are part of the essence of Catalonia and have become a true symbol of the region. The Greek and Roman civilisations brought wine production to the Mediterranean. Since then, the vines, vineyards and wineries have been a constant presence in the history and everyday life of Catalonia. As you wander through the villages in Catalonia you'll see that many late 17th- and 18th-century houses have the date they were built carved into the lintel above the door. Catalonia's inclusion on European trade routes, largely due to the demand for spirits from the United Kingdom and the Netherlands, and on American trade routes too, for spirits and other goods, brought great prosperity to rural communities, which still endures through the production of wine. When the phylloxera blight arrived in the late 19th century, it was a disaster for many counties. Catalan farmers who had been ruined by phylloxera were the first important group of incomers to settle in Barcelona. The beautiful cooperative wineries seen in many towns and villages in the south of Catalonia, many of them built in the art nouveau, or *modernista*, style, remind us that they were the rural world's answer to the wine crisis. There are wine trails that visit these interesting and spectacular wineries where you can also buy their finest wines and olive oils.

Today Catalonia has become Spain's leading producer of quality wines, with their own Designations of Origin (DO). The region produces more than 180 million bottles of wine and over 200 million bottles of 'cava' (a sparkling wine produced using the traditional method). Twelve DOs bear this out: Alella, Catalunya, Cava, Conca de Barberà, Costers del Segre, Empordà, Montsant, Penedès, Pla del Bages, Priorat (which holds the maximum quality distinction, DOQ), Tarragona and Terra Alta. In each of these areas, the geography, climate and grape varieties mean that Catalonia produces a wide variety of wines that have one thing in common: quality products obtained through a dedication and love of their growers and their desire to do better every day. Furthermore, in Catalonia, we have inherited the Greek and Roman tradition of making sweet wines from grape juice. The introduction of new grape varieties, including Malvasia and Moscatel, has allowed its wine-makers to produce wines of a pleasant, natural sweetness which are being enjoyed by more people and drunk more widely, not just with desserts but with other carefully made dishes.

Cities overlooking the sea

All along the beach-lined coast — the hypotenuse of the Catalan triangle — we find maritime cities: prosperous cities, open to the world, welcoming hosts of summer holidaymakers and tourists, which have had to supplement their trading and sailing tradition with tourism.

Heading up from the Ebro Delta towards Barcelona we follow the ancient Roman road, the Via Augusta. The main arteries running parallel to the coastal hypotenuse are nothing but variants of the Roman Via Augusta. Catalonia has many Roman archaeological remains and was home to one of the great provincial capitals of the Roman Empire: *Tarraco*, now the city of Tarragona. The province of Tarragona governed more than half the Iberian Peninsula.

Tarraco was a great Roman city. It is said to have been the biggest provincial capital of the Roman Empire. It is home to well-preserved relics of this period of splendour, inside the city (the theatre, amphitheatre, and circus, as befits a place of its standing at the time of the Empire) and its environs (the aqueduct, the villa and mausoleum of Centcelles, the villa of Els Munts, in Altafulla, the Mèdol quarry, the triumphal arch, the Arc de Berà, etc.). The Romans chose prime locations wherever they went and Tarragona is ample proof of this. When the city was no longer the Roman provincial capital, it retained the status of Christian ecclesiastical capital. Until 1969, the cardinal of Tarragona was the only one in Catalonia. This was seen as a tribute to the city's role as ecclesiastical capital, which was as ancient as Christianity on the Iberian Peninsula itself. It resulted in a splendid cathedral, which is the most spectacular one in Catalonia. Historically speaking, the ecclesiastical province of Tarragona is also the most stable territory in Catalonia.

You can feel Catalan diversity in the rivalry between the captivating city of Tarragona and neighbouring Reus. They both have a population of around 100,000 but the difference between them can be summed up as follows. Tarragona has always been a provincial or diocesan capital, large or small, at some point in its history, while Reus, a trading, industrious city, has never held this title but is known as an important trading hub where the spirit of commerce is still very much alive. Despite their proximity, the two cities have always led separate lives. Reus never used the port of Tarragona to export its fruit, wines and brandies, preferring to use the one in Salou instead.

Reus is the heir to Catalonia's prominence as a trading and industrial centre in the 18th, 19th and 20th centuries. It experienced, in a positive way, the phenomena of globalisation that developed over that long period, and was transformed from an agricultural capital to a commercial and financial capital. By the 19th century, Reus was a dynamic economic and business hub, and it came to be the second city in Catalonia, after Barcelona. It is also rich in architectural landmarks, and showcases some of the finest buildings from Catalonia's home-grown art nouveau movement, *modernisme*. Reus is the birthplace of the most influential Catalan politician of the contemporary era: General Joan Prim, the only one to be appointed president of the Council of Ministers, the only one to bring about the fall of a dynasty (the Bourbons) and usher in another (the House of Savoy). He was assassinated at the height of his career before he could welcome the new king of Spain, Amadeo of Savoy, who he had put on the throne. The brilliant painter Marià Fortuny was a contemporary of Prim's. He died relatively young but left behind a legacy of stunning works that never fail to impress. Antoni Gaudí is another illustrious figure from Reus. Although there are no works by Gaudí in his home town, the Catalan art nouveau, or *modernista* movement, left its imprint with some wonderful buildings, particularly those by Lluís Domènech i Montaner.

Other cities which resemble Reus in their economic, business and cultural development are Mataró, in the Maresme; Sitges and Vilanova i la Geltrú, in the Garraf; Sant Feliu de Guíxols, in the Baix Empordà; and Figueres, in the Alt Empordà (although it isn't on the coast, it has always turned its gaze to the sea). Mataró is the town that most closely resembles Reus economically speaking, but Sitges is the most unusual because, in the early 20th century, it attracted the intellectual and artistic elites of the time, who were bohemian yet well-off. Santiago Rusiñol was their leading light. He was from a family of industrialists and a great painter and writer who enjoyed great success throughout his career. Rusiñol built the mansion of Cau Ferrat in Sitges overlooking the sea and two beaches. The building encapsulates the most refined aesthetic tastes of the time: those of *modernisme*. This taste was rooted in the past and can be compared with Dalí's in Portlligat due to its spectacular location and professional approach. They resemble each other, yet are so different. Rusiñol was born in 1861 and fell in love with Sitges in 1891. The result, Cau Ferrat, is a building of extraordinary quality and sophistication that has nothing in common with Portlligat or Púbol Castle. Dalí was born in 1904 and fell in love with Portlligat in 1930. A true cultural and aesthetic revolution took place between the time of Rusiñol and Dalí, marking the distance between *modernisme* and surrealism.

Along the Costa Brava there are towns that have also been major trading hubs. Sant Feliu de Guíxols is traditionally known as the capital of the cork industry, and made its fortune from manufacturing corks for bottles in the 19th and much of the 20th centuries. The fine houses in Sant Feliu, its avenues, social clubs and harbour, remind us of the town's prosperity. It now has to compete with other emerging towns like Palamós, Platja d'Aro and Palafrugell. Much earlier, in medieval times, Sant Feliu was an insignificant place, and Castelló d'Empúries was the most important city on the coast of Girona. Nowadays it is a small town with a vast, lavishly decorated church which resembles a cathedral. For centuries, Castelló d'Empúries was the capital of the county that most fiercely resisted attempts to come under the rule of the House of Barcelona. The city reminds us that, a thousand years earlier, the Greek colony of Empúries stood nearby. It was the first city on the Catalan coast (the second, Roses, was a little further up on the other side of the gulf from which it takes its name). The Greek influence was diminished by the Romans, who, as we saw earlier, chose *Tarraco* as the centre of their Empire in Spain.

Barcelona, beginning and end

In the south, Sitges, Rusiñol and *modernisme* are nothing more than extensions of Barcelona. Barcelona's bourgeoisie used to spend the summer in their *modernista* villas in the towns in the Maresme, north-east of Barcelona. Heading inland, behind Barcelona, you'll find La Floresta, Valldoreix, Sant Cugat and other towns, and north-west of the city, Sabadell, Terrassa and Matadepera, which also bear the imprint of the creative prosperity of the early 20th century.

We've explored the three sides of the Catalan triangle and enjoyed a bird's-eye view of its centre of gravity, inland Catalonia. However, the true centre, the seat of power, is Barcelona, right in the middle of the hypotenuse. It is the most populous area, the birthplace of great initiatives and Catalonia's political and economic powerhouse. The capital of the Principality is, by definition, a constantly evolving, vibrant, urban, coastal city, with its own unique personality but also quintessentially Catalan, epitomising the region's liberal and creative essence, and a blend of all the

Catalonias you can imagine. The city is also the embodiment of Catalan diversity. In Barcelona you'll find fragments of everything you've already encountered in Catalonia.

You'll find Roman remains in other cities and towns. As a rule, they have enjoyed city or town status for the longest period of time: Badalona, Girona, Lleida, Mataró, Sabadell, Tarragona, Terrassa, Tortosa, Vic. The remains in Barcelona — formerly the Roman colony of *Barcino* — are in a good state of preservation and are well worth a leisurely visit.

Barcelona also has a wealth of Romanesque art and architecture, with churches like Sant Pau del Camp, an example of the purest Romanesque style, located inside the perimeter of the old town. There is also a Jewish Quarter which is gradually being restored (Barcelona had a large Jewish community in medieval times). In Barcelona we can see the development of the Gothic style, in religious buildings (the cathedral and the basilica of Santa Maria del Mar are the two main examples) and civil landmarks that are the pride of the city: the medieval shipyards, the Drassanes; the great hall, the Saló del Tinell, inside the former royal palace, the Palau Reial Major; the government chamber, the Saló del Consell de Cent; and the former commodities exchange, La Llotja…

However, there are few traces of Renaissance architecture in Barcelona and Catalonia, with the exception of Tortosa and a few others. We find many buildings from the baroque period as this was a time of great economic prosperity. However, most of the baroque sculptures were located in churches and lost during the Spanish Civil War (1936-1939), when many of them were burnt down. In Barcelona, the church of Betlem is the most prominent example of baroque architecture. Standing on La Rambla on the corner of Carrer del Carme, it has a unusual façade and wall on the side overlooking La Rambla.

The prosperity of the 19th century was represented by the neoclassical style in its different guises. The finest examples are on the Pla de Palau, where you'll find, side by side, a building from the late 18th century (first used as a customs house, then as the headquarters of the Captaincy General and later as the Office of the Spanish Government), the early 19th century (the Llotja de Mar which housed the Gothic commodities exchange), the mid-19th century (the colonnaded Porxos d'en Xifré), the late 19th century (the building that stands on the site of the old royal palace, that burnt down at Christmas 1875 and from which the square, the Plaça Reial, takes its name and the early 20th (the sailing school, the Escola de Nàutica), which all adhere to the classical cannon. The mansions on La Rambla are also neoclassical, as is the new façade of Barcelona City Hall.

Modernisme is the architectural style that can be found throughout Catalonia, and has come to be recognised as a national style. In the late 19th century and the first decades of the 20th in particular, the creativity of the *modernista* movement had a major impact on the architectural scene. Barcelona was at the forefront, as is shown by the plethora of buildings throughout the Eixample neighbourhood. Antoni Gaudí's Sagrada Família is the most famous and popular with visitors. Throughout Catalonia (and on the Balearic Islands, which it is culturally very close to) there was a particular fashion for building *modernista*-style industrial buildings, from factories to wineries and oil mills. This was no passing fad and we find examples of *modernista* industrial architecture throughout the region, which have become symbols of its cultural and national identity. They date from the time when Catalan prosperity was probably at its height.

Barcelona is also full of buildings and sculptures from the *noucentista* period. *Noucentisme* came about as a reaction to *modernisme* and neo-Gothic and Romantic Historicism with a return to a more classical style, a longing for a cultural renewal that had never come about, and a desire for greater rationalism. Plaça de Catalunya and

Via Laietana, Plaça d'Espanya and Montjuïc hill were all laid out according to the *noucentista* ethos, from 1910 to 1930. The financial crisis and the Civil War left few traces of art deco in Barcelona, but you'll still find some valuable examples.

All these traditions continued with eclectic architecture, which was able to adapt to its urban surroundings, until the reinstatement of a democratically elected municipal council, and the Olympic Games reinvented Barcelona's public space as we know it today. We are, of course, referring to town planning as well as architecture and great sculptures.

Barcelona has always had a life of its own, but now it has more life than ever. What makes the city tick is no longer true for the rest of Catalonia. Its global expansion, best expressed through the massive, year-round influx of tourists from all over the world, has shifted the goalposts. Business headquarters and government offices have gradually moved out of the centre and it has become a vast retail showcase. Fewer and fewer Catalans go there on everyday business, and prefer it as a place for shopping and sightseeing, like tourists do.

This is quite odd because Barcelona hadn't shown much interest in tourists. It was a city of trade fairs and congresses. An industrial, trading city, the centre of many industrial districts made up of small and medium-sized businesses. Trade fairs and congresses were its pole of attraction for visitors and nobody stayed on at weekends to go sightseeing. The hotels had to offer discounts to attract holidaymakers and people on weekend breaks. It was similar to Hamburg, Rotterdam, Marseilles, Genoa and Liverpool, to give a few European examples. They were all industrial and industrious port cities. Their ambition was to resemble the wealthiest industrial and trading inland cities, like Milan, Lyon and Munich.

The change began with the reinstatement of democratic municipal councils who guided Barcelona's new elites towards the concerns of the community: more parks, more public amenities, better town planning, and an ambition to improve. During Franco's time, the municipal elite had shredded the city, destroying countless beautiful buildings and mansions and replacing them with eyesores. Despite its focus on property development and speculation, during the second half of the dictatorship, the city also nursed an ambition to be a metropolitan centre. The then mayor persuaded Franco to draw up a municipal charter for Barcelona that gave it privileged legal and economic status that, while not comparable with Madrid, set it apart from other Spanish cities. Indeed, during his tenure from 1957 to 1972, the mayor Porcioles imagined and designed Barcelona for the next generation, bringing in skilled and ambitious young architects and planners. The only proviso was that they showed loyalty to their city. The result was a town-planning scheme that formed the basis of the Olympic Barcelona of 1992 and the post-Olympic city, which is still being completed. When Narcís Serra (the first democratically elected mayor after the reinstatement of democracy) and his successor, Pasqual Maragall, took advantage of the fact that the president of the International Olympic Committee, Juan Antonio Samaranch, also hailed from Barcelona and was willing to launch a discreet, yet effective, campaign to secure the Olympics for the city, the entire population was mobilised and the city won its bid in October 1986. Barcelona changed completely for the 1992 Olympic Games and has never stopped changing and improving since then.

Some of the changes are totally novel. There is a lot of innovative architecture and a great many smart buildings, but there is even more protection for buildings, and the city's existing heritage is being restored. The cleaning of the façades was the first revolution. Highlighting the value of the *modernista* heritage, the legitimate heir to the taste of the Catalan bourgeoisie who got rich on the back of Catalan industrialisation during the 19th century, was the next step. A Barcelona that came to like itself more and more, multiplied its cultural and architectural initiatives. In the midst of an economy in crisis, Barcelona was able to position itself as a social and business reference point. During years of plenty, the refurbishments and reconversions multiplied of their own accord, under the watchful eye of Barcelona's municipal elite.

Along the way, the city has opened to the sea — the first major change —, landscaped areas have been created, avenues and boulevards have been opened up and developed, major museums have opened, and countless buildings have been restored and put to other uses. The city has attracted professionals from abroad to live and work there and its metropolitan transport network — which is always highly praised by visitors — has been expanded. In keeping with the city's tolerant and Mediterranean mindset, Barcelona has become fashionable.

Barcelona has become the city of Gaudí and *modernisme*, a showcase of history and culture, of attractive shops, cutting-edge gastronomy, pavement cafés, shops open all day, great public services, a joie de vivre, an excellent standard of living for its residents, as well as Barça, urban beaches, bikes that are finding their place among the dense traffic, of marinas, of all the landscapes that are less than two hours' drive away. It has become a competitor with Paris and London.

Barcelona is the embodiment of coexistence and diversity. Taking this diversity on board has been vital to restoring confidence to Barcelona and Catalonia. Barcelona's successes have always been a concern for those politicians doing their utmost to make Catalonia a place with its own distinct identity. It seemed that the world only knew Catalonia as the land of Barcelona. Barcelona was becoming the international identity of Catalonia. Put even more simply, on a planetary scale, we could say that Barça (FC Barcelona) used to represent the identity of Catalonia around the world.

This would have continued had it not been for Catalonia's call for independence, which has put the "Catalonia" brand firmly on the world map. It has bolstered its image, unintentionally but successfully. We'll discuss all of this — Barcelona, Barça, *modernisme*, the Catalans, their desire for independence — in other books in the same collection.

Find out more

The excellent Wikipedia entry on Catalonia is an essential starting point to find out about the region.

The best introduction to Catalonia is Robert Hughes' book *Barcelona* (Harvill, London, 1992; Random House, New York, 1992) which has been translated into different languages. It is really more of an essay about Catalonia and nothing else compares with it or has enjoyed the same success. The book was written to tell the readers what was interesting about the city that was going to host the 1992 Olympic Games, and Hughes managed to create a unique summary of Catalonia. His initial aim was to explain Gaudí's work, but his exploration and interpretation of Catalonia's history and way of life remains unsurpassed.

Two splendid (and short) books look at Catalonia from a German viewpoint: *Catalunya vista per un alemany*, by Til Stegmann (La Campana, Barcelona, 1988, which has been republished many times), and *Katalonien – eine kleine Landeskunde*, by Klaus-Jürgen Nagel (Messidor Verlag, Stuttgart, 2007). The first was written by a Catalonia enthusiast, a German who lived in Barcelona as a child for family reasons, who rediscovered Catalonia as an adult. It is written for Catalans through the eyes of a friendly outsider. The second was presented to the German public at the 2007 Frankfurt Book Fair, which was dedicated to Catalonia.

The Catalan government, the Generalitat de Catalunya, published a large-format book entitled *Conèixer Catalunya (Conocer Cataluña / Getting to Know Catalonia / Connaissance de la Catalogne / Katalonien Kennenlernen)*, by Josep Maria Puigjaner, in a number of editions from 2000 to 2003. It is available from the Catalan government's online bookshop.

The best illustrated guide is *Catalunya* by Sebastià Roig, (Triangle Books, Sant Lluís, Menorca), which is published in several languages and in a large or small format.

Index

TRIANGLE▼BOOKS